MANAGING LIFE'S STRESS

"LEARNING EFFECTIVE STRESS MANAGEMENT STRATEGIES TO ENRICH YOUR LIFE"

By

DANIEL J. RANDALL

Dedication

I dedicate this book first to my wife Linda, who took the time to just listen and in doing so, helped me to get started on releasing the demons that had been within me for nearly 20 years. I didn't even know they were there until one night that became known as "***Deck Night***". I also dedicate this to my sons Jamison and Chad. I am very proud of both of these young men, and I thank them for their love.

Acknowledgements

I would like to thank the following for taking the time to review this book and provide me with their honest and sincere critiques and encouragements: my wife Linda, sister-in-law Joan Randall, brother-in-law Roger Madden and cousin Lynnette Welsch. Without their help, this book might not have been completed. I thank you all and truly appreciate your input and support.

Table of Contents

Introduction

Stress is an intrical part of our lives and is something that we must learn to manage. We can not wish it away, nor do we want to. Stress can make our lives more exciting and enjoyable. Normally we think of stress as a negative in our lives. In choosing to read this book, you are taking a step in the right direction to improve your own well being. Not everything in this book will apply to you. Highlight those things that touch you or seem relevant. After you have finished the book, go back and review the highlighted areas. Make a plan to take action and start reducing your stress on a daily basis. Like playing a musical instrument or excelling in a sport, getting proficient in managing stress and getting your life under control will take some practice. There are quick fixes for some types of stress, but other stress that is deeply embedded inside of us will take some time and work to make the necessary changes.

My road to recovery started when I was 34 years old and, at the time, I had no clue that I even had stress. On the contrary, I thought my life was going like gang busters and all was well with Dan Randall. What I learned was that I was suppressing thoughts, emotions and memories that were tearing me apart from the inside. I was home one evening with my family when I began to feel some tingling and numbness in the fingers and toes. I then started sweating and got the chills. Next came the shortness of breath, tightness and pain in the chest area. I was sure I was having a heart attack. I asked my wife to call my doctor and tell him what was happening. When he told her that I wasn't having a heart attack and that it was an anxiety attack, I got on the phone and started arguing with him. "How can you tell me it's not a heart attack when you aren't here to see what is happening to me." He responded, "If you were having a heart attack, you wouldn't be arguing with me on the phone. You would be lying on the floor in pain." He told me to relax and start taking some slow, deep breaths into a paper bag. Considering the way I treated him, I'm surprised he didn't tell me to use a plastic bag. We set up an appointment for the next morning. It was a very long night of slow breathing and lots of praying.

When I got to see my doctor, I quickly explained that I couldn't have stress as everything was going great in my life. I had a loving wife, two healthy sons, a nice home in a good community and a dream job doing something I loved for a major company that could offer me long time stability. I was even recently promoted and got to travel around the world. What could be better? My doctor also happened to be my wife's cousin and he had lots of family history on me. So we started to talk. He reminded me that I had experienced a number of deaths in my family. There was James, a baby brother, who had died at 6 months of pneumonia. Then Kathleen, our sister who died at age 9 of leukemia. She was then followed by my brother Robert at age 38 of lupus and then just a year prior to my attack, my dad died at 66 of cancer. I said, "yeah, OK, so I have family who has died. We are all going to die, and it is just part of the cycle. Right?"

He then said, "I know you served with the Marines in Vietnam. Why don't you tell me about that experience?" I responded, "No, I don't want to talk about that. People don't want to hear about Vietnam. It was bad enough coming home to protesters who would spit at you and they and others would call you names like baby killer. No, I don't think I want to talk about that." Then he said, "OK, tell me about this new job". I said, "It's great. I get to travel all over the world." My doctor then asked how my family feels about my being gone so much. Sometimes I'm gone for three to five weeks at a time and I know it is tough on them. I guess I feel a little guilty for leaving everything in my wife's hands. I do miss her and the boys, but that is my job and it gives us the money to have the things we need.

At this point he told me that I am harboring anger, bitterness, remorse, frustration, and other emotions that are breaking me down from the inside. If you don't start dealing with these feelings, the next time it will be a heart attack instead of an anxiety attack. You need to start now to get this under control. So that's when it all started and I began to research and apply stress management techniques into my daily life. Over the next four years I studied books, articles, attended seminars and conferences and applied what I had learned. The big breakthrough came in 1986 during "**Deck Night**", which I'll talk about in Chapter IV.

Here are the benefits you will get from learning how to gain control over your stress.

- more control over your life
- able to connect better with other people
- gain an improved sense of meaning and purpose
- lower blood pressure
- improved disposition
- reduce wear and tear on your body and mind
- change your attitude from "have to" to "want to"
- a positive improvement in overall wellness

I hope you find this book enlightening and more importantly, useful. I hope you find the one piece of information that starts you on your road to recovery and well being.

Remember, the information provided in this book is a result of my own research and application in my life. If you are experiencing severe stress, you should consult your doctor or a professional medical service.

———

Chapter I:
Stress Management – The Basics

Simply put, stress is what happens to our bodies when demands are made of it. There are many definitions of stress, however, I would rather explain it with the **Three Steps of Stress**.

- First is the situation or event that causes the mind to know there is stress
- Second are the thoughts we had about the situation or event
- Third is the action we take from those thoughts we had about the situation or event

The most important of these steps is our thoughts about the situation or event. With positive thoughts, we can turn a bad situation into good. Consider the plight of a man from Minnesota who lost both his legs in an accident. He could have let that event destroy him. He could have been angry and depressed and given up on living. Instead, he made a decision that he wanted to live and take his life back. He developed a plan for his recovery and with the help of family and friends he followed through with that plan. The results were nothing less than phenomenal. Within five months he was walking on artificial legs and in six months he was golfing. After seven months he was back to work and a year later started a not-for-profit organization which now helps others who have lost arms or legs to get back their lives.

There are two distinct types of stress. They are "*acute*" and "*chronic*". Acute is that every day stress we experience and is usually short lived. We can normally use basic stress management techniques, covered in Chapter IV, to make these go away. Examples that cause acute stress are: waking up late for work, getting a flat tire, driving in heavy traffic jams, dealing with an irate customer or snappy sales clerk. Acute stress can also come from an exhilarating ski run or while whitewater rafting. Make a list of those every day situations that cause you stress.

Chronic stress is difficult to get under control, but certainly not impossible. <u>Chronic stress results from long term exposure to acute stress that is left uncared for.</u> If waking up late becomes a daily habit, it could ultimately cause more serious problems like job loss. When insults continue day after day and no action is taken to halt them, resolving this issue will be much more difficult. Other forms of chronic stress include: major illnesses, abuse during childhood or as an adult, relationship problems, major financial or work issues.

We hear reports about post traumatic stress disorder (PTSD) and how it affects our military personnel. The first known article on stress was written in a medical journal in 1916. It related to issues our soldiers were having when coming home from WWI. Not much has changed. Think about the similarities and problems military personnel have experienced during and after WWII, Korean War, Cuban Crisis, Vietnam War, Desert Storm, Kuwait, Iran, Iraq or Afghanistan. Nor can we forget about the affects these wars have on family and friends. Serving in the military during a war is not the only cause of <u>PTSD</u>. People can suffer as a result of divorce, death in the family, birth of a child, or even after a car accident. <u>Any traumatic event in our lives can cause this condition.</u> We'll discuss more about types of stress in Chapter II.

Chart A below shows a normal stress response cycle. Notice the four points marked along the curve that our bodies follow when stress occurs. Imagine that you and a close friend are walking through a nature preserve. It's a beautiful morning in late spring, flowers are in full bloom. The sun is bright and warm with a clear blue sky. You are in the normal stress free zone (1). Then, about 20 yards in front of you, a very large bear jumps out on the pathway. At this point, your mind tells the body that it needs to take action. It immediately jumps up to the stress zone (2). Here the mind starts to take charge and automatically prepares you for what is commonly referred to as the "flight or fight" mode. In this condition the body reacts in a particular manner. Among the changes that occur are the tightening of the diaphragm, blood pressure and pulse rates go up, breathing becomes faster and not as deep, blood is pushed to the muscles and the immune system weakens.

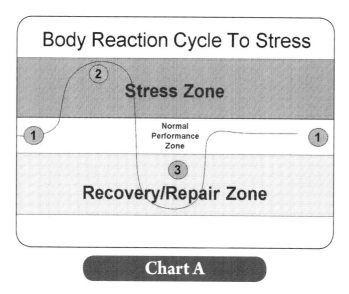

Chart A

You and your friend make a quick decision to run like a deer to get away. Soon you look around and you are safe from the bear. Once the threat is over, your body starts to go back to normal. However, it doesn't stop in this zone. Instead it drops into the recovery and repair zone (3) so that it can fix the things that were damaged in the stress zone (2). Once repaired, you move back into the normal zone (1) until the next situation. Pretty simple to understand, isn't it? By the way, if you do run into a bear, remember that you don't have to out run the bear. You only have to out run your friend!

If this is all there was, it wouldn't be so tough. However, life isn't that simple. In Chart B below we see what is probably a more typical day for most. There are a series of events which bring on stress throughout the day. If you look closely, we aren't always able to get into the recovery and repair zone (3) to fix our bodies before going right back into the stress zone (2). If this has occurred several times throughout the day, it's no wonder we are exhausted by the end of the day. If this continues for days, weeks or months, we can become quite ill and in need of professional medical help.

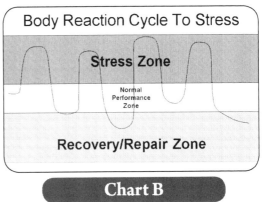

Chart B

Excess stress can result in burnout. If you experience any of the following, seek help immediately.

- Chronic fatigue
- Cynicism and negativity
- A sense of being besieged
- Exploding easily at seemingly inconsequential things
- Frequent headaches and gastrointestinal problems
- Feeling of helplessness
- Increased degree of risk taking

———————

Chapter II:
Sources of Stress

In this chapter, we look at eight categories of stress and provide examples of events that may cause stress. Why does it seem that we have more stress today than in the past? The world is changing rapidly and becoming faster paced. We are exposed to real time happenings from around the world. Prior to addressing each category, let's take a moment and look at how situations in just one area of our lives have changed.

While attending a church service near Milwaukee, a guest speaker was talking about how schools have changed over the past 60 years. The information he shared could point to why we have more stress today than in the past. The speaker spoke about the top seven issues affecting school administrators during the 1940's versus 2006. Here are the results beginning with the seventh rated issue.

1940	2006
7. Not putting gum in trash.	7. Assaults
6. Wearing improper clothing	6. Robbery
5. Getting out of turn in line	5. Rape
4. Running in hallways	4. Suicide
3. Making noise in hallways	3. Teen pregnancy
2. Chewing gum	2. Alcohol abuse
1. Talking in class	1. Drug abuse

There is a growing trend in the United States for young people to mutilate themselves by cutting or burning their legs, thighs or arms. When they cut or burn themselves, endorphins are released into the body. Endorphins are our body's natural pain killer and can be three times stronger than morphine. The teenagers reasoning is that they have control over the pain they are giving to themselves whereas they do not have control over the pain they are getting through emotional and mental abuses in their lives.

Another troubling trend is the increase in teenagers who are getting sexually transmitted diseases. There are many studies which indicate that 1 in 4 teenage girls have an STD. In addition, every 24 hours over 2,700 teenage girls will get pregnant. We do live in a different world and we must try to understand and help resolve these issues.

Visual media is exposing us and our children to sights and sounds we were never able to see or hear with such ease. Unfortunately much of what we see and hear today is dangerous. Video games have gone from Pac Man to games which promote sexual assaults on women, murder, and even cop killing. Certain websites show boys and girls in one on one street fights and groups of school age children beating up on one person. Sometimes the parents are there watching and encouraging their children. Vulgarity is heard on the airwaves every minute of the day. Even popular celebrities think nothing of using four letter expletives on prime time TV. Yes, times have changed, and with it more exposure to stressful situations.

Eight categories of stress.

1. Any life change or important event -
   a. Death of a loved one
   b. Divorce
   c. Major health issues
   d. Experiencing war
   e. Job loss
   f. Marriage
   g. Retirement
   h. Career change
   i. Having a baby
   j. Moving – buying or selling your home
   k. Company reorganization resulting in reassignment
   l. Empty nest
   m. Mid-life
   n. Heading to college
   o. First date
   p. First kiss
   q. Vacation

In the list above the first five examples could cause a significantly higher stress level than the others, but each person will react differently during a similar event or change. ***How we view situations determines the amount of stress we will have.***

The experience of being in a war can cause a traumatic affect on our minds causing a separation between the left and right brain functions. This disconnect can take years of professional help to link the two together again. One key to surviving is to talk about what is going on in your head with someone who can support you. Do not let it fester and destroy you from the inside. War is not the only situation which can cause trauma to this extent. Rape, assaults, near death experiences, and even having a baby have been known to result in what is known as PTSD or post traumatic stress disorder. You can survive this with help.

2. Threats to our person or self-esteem -
   a. Bullying or harassment
   b. Assault (including domestic abuse)
   c. Robbery
   d. Talk of job layoffs

At first I didn't see how getting bullied or harassed was such a big deal. Now I realize that getting bullied today is much different from when I grew up. In my school days we might get bullied at the bus stop before or after school. Sometimes this might end with a punch in the nose. However, we really didn't see much of this once we were on the bus or at school. Back then bus drivers and teachers were given not only the responsibility, but the authority to discipline bad behavior. Today, attempts to do this could end up in a law suit against the bus driver or teacher. With the technology we have today children not only get bullied and harassed in person, but via instant messaging, text messaging, email and on social networks. It's constant and impossible for them to get away from it. Today that punch may be an attack with a knife or gun and not just a fist. It is estimated that 50,000 teenagers attempt suicide each year and many do so because of the constant harassment they are getting from their peers. Five thousand of those who attempt suicide succeed.

Layoffs are occurring at an alarming rate with talks of recession heard on a daily basis as stock prices fluctuate. Housing foreclosures are at their highest level in many years, and businesses are reducing staff just to try and survive the market challenges.

It is also extremely frightening to think that as many as one in three women who are in relationships with men are being mentally, emotionally or physically abused. For help in this area call 1-800-799-7233 for the National Domestic Violence Helpline or just call 911.

3. Loss of someone or something we care for or depend on -

    a. Spouse
    b. Child
    c. Other family member
    d. Family pet
    e. Home
    f. Job
    g. Photos

It's obvious that losing a spouse or child is devastating, but the loss of a family pet can be very devastating too. Those who have no children often care for and relate to their pets as if they are family and they too need to go through the grieving process. If you listen to a TV interview of people after they have lost a home to fire or other disaster, you will often hear them say they have lost everything. This includes their family photos which are tangible memories.

Next to my house, I had a favorite tree located only 20 feet from my back deck. It was a blue spruce about 40 feet tall and just perfect in shape. I would watch it grow each year and each year it would become more beautiful. One day I noticed some debris under the tree. I got down on my hands and knees and crawled under the tree to clean it up. Once under the tree I noticed something amazing. This beautiful blue spruce, which had grown so tall and so perfect in shape, wasn't a blue spruce after all. It was in fact two blue spruces that had been growing side by side all these years. Each tree was giving up part of its space and allowing the other tree to grow and thrive. As I looked at it, I thought that this is what a perfect relationship is all about. Two people living together, each giving ground, and allowing the other to grow and thrive to make one perfect union.

A couple of years later a strong straight line wind came through and tore the trees' roots from the ground and caused the trees to topple. There was nothing I could do to save them. I had to hire a landscaping company to come and remove the trees from my yard. For the next year I would walk out to my deck and look to where the trees once stood. I would remember how beautiful they were and how much pleasure and joy they gave me. I literally missed them and was sad for the loss. Then it happened. One day I went out to my deck and stared at where my special trees once beautified my yard. Suddenly, my eyes shifted beyond the 20 feet in front of me where the trees once grew, and I could see for miles. It seemed that the trees, as beautiful as they were, were blocking my view of a lovely valley now in sight. I still miss those trees, but I now love my new view. So when tragedy strikes and takes something or someone from you, be patient, as in time you may just find something or someone to start filling the hole left by your loss.

4. Conflicting or unclear demands or expectations -
   a. Expectations not defined
   b. Time lines not defined
   c. Responsibility and accountability without authority or support

In the hectic and fast-paced world we live today, those who are in charge i.e., supervisors, managers, parents, teachers, sergeants, generals, politicians are often so busy trying to keep up with their own demands and lives, that they don't make the time to pass down what they expect from those who report to them or look to them for direction. This leaves us to question what is really expected of us or when we are expected to have things done to meet deadlines.

Some workers i.e., laborers, production line employees and some low level management, work with great responsibility and accountability, but are given little if any decision making authority or support.

5. Pressures of deadlines/too much work/confused priorities -
    a. Sales quota
    b. Home responsibilities
    c. Work responsibilities
    d. Educational responsibilities
    e. Social responsibilities
    f. Personal needs

Anyone who has worked in a sales position knows that their weekly/monthly/quarterly quotas never go down. Once a quota is met, the next expectation is that the new quota is going to be higher and the next and the next. There is no break from it. If we look at all of the activities that make up our lives, we have to wonder how we can fit everything in. Where do our priorities lie? This will sound selfish to some people, but I firmly believe that we have to put the priority on our own wellness first before any other aspect of our life. The reason I believe this is that if we are not well ourselves, how can we fulfill our obligations in other aspects of our lives?

I keep remembering what the flight attendants repeat over and over again on every flight of every airline in the world. "If there is loss of cabin pressure during the flight, oxygen masks will drop down from the overhead compartment in front of you. ***Pull down the mask and place it on yourself first, before attempting to assist others***."

Think about it. It makes sense.

6. Conflict or difficulty with other people -

a. Family members
b. Friends
c. Work associates
d. School Board or PTA
e. Church committees
f. Sales clerk or wait staff
g. Customer service representative on the phone
h. Impatient or irate customers

Much of the time, the issues we have with others are generally due to misunderstandings caused by poor or misinterpreted communications. Chart C, on the next page, shows two types of communicators.

The "*rapport*" talker is one who needs to provide the listener with substantial detail and personal information before they ever get to the point of the conversation. The "*report*" talker, on the other hand, gets right to the point and will only share personal information or details about the topic if they are asked for it.

I, for example, am a "report" person. This came very clear one day when I was sending out an email to my co-workers to tell them that I had just become a new grandfather. My email consisted of the following: "Hi everyone, just wanted to let you know that as of this morning, I became a grandfather. Have a good day - Dan". That was it. What more is there to say? Within minutes, I had 5 people standing at my cubicle door asking all of the other questions. "Was it a boy or girl; what is the baby's name; what time was it born; how much did it weigh; how long was it; how is the mother and dad doing? So many questions…I knew all the answers, but didn't know why they needed to know. Silly me. Rapport people need to know!

Communicate Clearly

Rapport Talk vs. **Report Talk**

Details / Personal / Bottom of the pyramid

Top of the pyramid / Get to the point / Non-personal

Adapt your communication to the way your listener wants to communicate

Chart C

There is another type comparison that I learned about one day when my wife and I went to a counselor to get advice on our marriage. During our session our counselor was telling us about "*linear*" and "*cyclical*" types. Linear are those who when hit with a problem or issue, address it, handle it in some manner and then move on. A cyclical person in the same situation may revisit the problem or issue in a day, in a week or even a year later. Hearing this was like a lightning bolt hitting me. It clarified many issues that had come up in our marriage and why we sometimes have communication problems. According to my wife, I became a better husband after this session because I better understood why she was reacting differently than I had to the same situation. So are you a rapport or a report person and are you linear or cyclical? It makes a huge difference, and learning how to communicate to someone of the opposite type can change your life and your stress level.

Here's some very interesting information about communications that came from the book <u>The Five Love Languages</u>. <u>How we communicate our love or caring for someone should be said in a manner our loved ones want to hear.</u> As a husband, father, family member, friend, co-worker, etc., I am a doer. I do things for people to show that I love them or care about them. I don't necessarily say the words people want to hear because I think by doing something for them lets them know how I feel. This is not necessarily the case. <u>Because if the other people are sayers, then my doing does not register with them. They need to hear the words that I love or care for them and no matter how much I do, it will never be enough.</u> It's not saying that they don't appreciate what I do for them, it just isn't providing them what they need to really know that I care. <u>And for those who are sayers, trying to communicate their love or caring to a doer, their words will not be enough either. Hearing I love you makes a doer say...yeah, I know, but what have you done for me lately?</u> *You need to know who you are talking with and then make the most of that relationship by communicating in the manner that the other person needs to hear.*

7. Threats to our needs -

There are four basic needs each human requires in order to survive. These are air, food, water and shelter. I contend there is a 5th element each of us needs and that is hope. There are events that happen in our lives that directly affect each of these elements.

a. Drop in the stock market
b. Talks of recession
c. Prices on the rise
d. Global warming
e. Terror attacks
f. Housing foreclosures
g. Pollution

Certainly financial security is a primary need for which we all strive. In times of stock market uncertainty, dollar devaluation, gas, food and most other items taking a sharp trend upwards, we get very nervous about our financial future and even our financial present. We also have a need to be safe. Since September 11, 2001, the constant fear of another attack in the world against innocent people has us on edge still today. The constant reminder from the news media 24/7 doesn't help the situation. These are just a few of the things which can poke holes in the hope we have for our future. Don't let them ruin your life. It seems like we never get enough time to take care of ourselves, and it is important to make that time. Don't rely on your annual vacation to relieve stress – start building in daily prevention. This will help you deal with the adversity that affects your needs.

8. Self -

   a. Perception to an event can be more stressful than the event itself

   Our mind does not differentiate between a real stressful event and the perception we have about that event. In many cases, we have a tendency to perceive stressful situations which might happen. In her book, Breaking Free from Stress, Linda Mintle PHD states that 70 - 90% of visits to physicians' offices are stress-related. Other research indicates that nearly 90% of doctor's visits stem from our perception of what might happen that causes us a stress related illness, but these events never happen. We find ourselves in the "what if" mode of thinking and we almost always think the worst case scenario. As stated earlier in this book, a large part of our stress is a matter of perception. ***How you view a situation determines how much*** ✕ ✕ ***stress you will have.*** Yes, I know this is the second time that I have used this statement. I think it is that important.

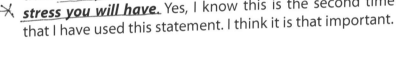

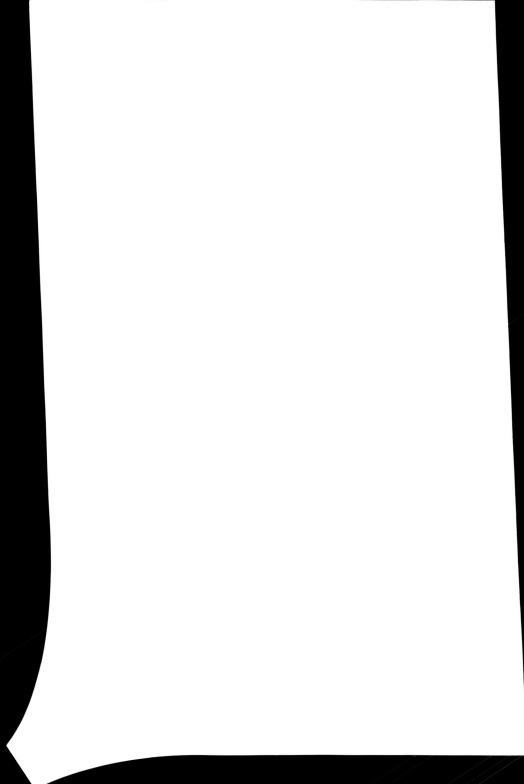

Chapter III:
Symptoms of Stress

This chapter addresses the symptoms that occur when we are under stressful situations, which are categorized as physical, emotional, mental, behavioral and organizational. Each category identifies the symptoms and provides explanations for some examples.

1. Physical Symptoms -
   a. Headache
   b. Dry mouth
   c. Grinding teeth
   d. Pupils dilate
   e. Difficult, shallow breathing
   f. Heartburn
   g. Muscle tension
   h. Digestive system slows
   i. Numbness
   j. Queasy stomach
   k. Sweating
   l. Tingling and coldness in the extremities
   m. Back pain
   n. Increased adrenaline, blood sugar, heart rate and blood pressure

Let's examine some of the most common physical symptoms. Most people know that speaking in front of a large group is stressful, and dry mouth is one of the most common symptoms that occur to speakers. That's why speakers and talk show hosts will have a bottle or cup of water near by.

Grinding of the teeth often occurs during the night while we're sleeping. If you notice someone doing this, you might want to ask them if they have some concerns they want to talk about.

Did you know that when someone lies, their pupils dilate? If you're not sure that someone is telling you the truth, look into their eyes.

If you eat three chili dogs, you could very well get heartburn. But, if you're getting heartburn without a known accelerant, it could be stress related.

Driving a car in heavy traffic or bad weather can cause our hands to grip the wheel too tightly, make our shoulders rise up into our necks, make our stomach tighten and cause our legs to pull together. All of these cause muscle tension.

2. Emotional Symptoms -

   a.   Anger, bitterness and unforgiveness
   b.   Anxiety and frustration
   c.   Boredom and fatigue
   d.   Depression and withdrawal from reality
   e.   Moodiness
   f.   Nervousness
   g.   Self-criticism
   h.   Worry

From time to time everyone gets angry, bitter and frustrated with things happening around them or with people they encounter. Anger and bitterness are two of the emotions which festered inside me from the time I returned from Vietnam in 1969 until that day in 1986 when I finally started to let the demons out. There are acceptable ways to release these feelings and unacceptable ways to release them. I was not using acceptable ways of releasing these emotions. As a matter of fact, I wasn't releasing them at all. Negative feelings may start in the brain, but they quickly engulf the entire body. Anger is natural. Learning to express your anger constructively and let it go is a key to keeping healthy. Which are you choosing? Chapter IV will show you some stress reduction tips to relieve stress symptoms in an acceptable way.

   Depression is a state where we have given up the will to continue. It is very difficult to recover from this condition alone. Someone with depression might say things like "I feel sad all of the time" or "I don't enjoy doing the things I use to do or be with people I used to enjoy being with". They might also say "Sometimes I feel like my life isn't worth living anymore". It is not something that you should feel embarrassed, ashamed about or take lightly.

Depression is among the leading causes of disability worldwide with women more than twice as likely as men to experience depression. People with family history, chronic or debilitating medical conditions or those experiencing a major life change, even a joyous one like becoming a new parent, are susceptible to this disease.

Thoughts about death and suicide are common in depression. It is important to take such thoughts seriously. If you feel like giving up or if you might hurt yourself, get help immediately. Call your doctor, go to the emergency room, call 911 or call the National Suicide Prevention Helpline @ 1-800-784-2433 or 1-800-SUICIDE.

3. Mental Symptoms -
a. Can't turn off certain thoughts
b. Defensiveness
c. Difficulty concentrating
d. Insomnia
e. Mental blocks
f. Poor task performance
g. Problems focusing on details

We all forget things, mess things up, have a hard time staying on task and we sometimes attribute these to the onset of Alzheimer's or maybe a senior moment. In most cases it is simply that we are under pressure, have too many things to do and in a stressful situation at the moment. When things calm down, these symptoms usually go away. If they don't, then we have to look to professional help to assist in sorting them out and finding the cause.

Insomnia or having difficulty falling asleep happens to all of us at some point and it is often because we have too many things on our minds that worry us. If relaxation techniques discussed in this book do not work, please get professional medical consultation.

4. Behavioral Symptoms -
   a. Prone to accidents
   b. Blaming others
   c. Physical or chemical abuse
   d. Impulsive or aggressive outbursts
   e. Loss of appetite or overeating
   f. Loss of sexual desire
   g. Restlessness
   h. Isolation and withdrawal

The wear and tear on our body is caused not by stress alone, but also the unhealthy habits developed in response to the stress i.e. smoking, drinking, drugs, self mutilation, abuse to others.

When I visited a middle school and talked with eighth graders, I was hit square in the face with some frightening facts about what teenagers are dealing with and what drastic measures they go through to release their stress. A number of students indicated in a survey that they were or knew someone who was burning or cutting themselves to relieve the mental and emotional stress they had. They said they did so because the physical pain was something they had control over, whereas the mental and emotional stress was something they could not control. In studies it has been learned that young people are even joining groups and having cutting and burning parties.

They become their own special click of fellow sufferers. One site to get information about cutting is ***www.christiananswers.net***. After getting the site, search cutting (go) and then scroll down to 1. Help for cutters.

As indicated earlier, we each react to stressors in different ways. Some of us when in a stressful situation will stop eating while others will overeat. Some of us will have impulsive outbursts while others will withdraw and isolate themselves from others.

5. Organizational Symptoms -
   a. Absenteeism
   b. Accidents
   c. High turnover
   d. High use of health facilities
   e. Job burnout
   f. Job dissatisfaction
   g. Lawsuits
   h. Low morale
   i. Poor performance
   j. Poor working relationships

High use of health facilities does not mean visiting Curves or Anytime Fitness. It means doctors and clinic visits. As previously stated, based on studies at a number of universities, it is estimated that 70% - 90% of all doctor and clinic visits are stress related. The first I ever heard of job burnout was back during President Reagan's term of office and the U.S. experienced the Air Traffic Controller's strike. The claim was that long hours and intense job responsibilities were causing a high level of burnout among the controllers. I don't know about you, but I don't want those men and women getting burned out while I'm in the air.

So is there anything good about stress?

Absolutely!

Stress challenges us to excel

It will not prevent us from working productively

It helps us be more alert

It increases our motivation and drive

It can be channeled to increase performance levels.

Chapter IV:
Stress Reduction Tips

- The very first tip I can give you is to be aware of the signs of stress as talked about in Chapter III. Once you recognize that you are in a stressful situation, you can take appropriate action to start recovering from it. Learn the warning signs and then take action.
- The next tip is to find and then not be afraid to use one of the many resources available through your place of worship, school, place of employment, in your community or even on-line via the Internet. You don't get extra points, as a matter of fact, you don't get any points for trying to fix everything yourself. Ask for help. You can always start with a friend. Today, we seem to have fewer friends than 10 or 15 years ago, primarily because we have less time to cultivate friendships. But use the friends you do have and talk to them about your concerns and problems. If you don't feel comfortable going to a friend, then search out someone you can and do trust. You might consider someone at your place of worship. Try calling a member of the law enforcement agency or someone in the medical field. Look in the yellow pages for professional services that might be available in your community. If you are or were in the military, check out your American Legion or VFW for assistance. The important thing is that you should not stop looking until you find someone who can help.
- I've had many people come to me and say "Gee, I want to attend your program because I know I can

use it, but I'm just too busy to come". To these people I say "STOP". The next tip is to slow down and take time to plan. Slow down you say? I've got too much to do to slow down. This is exactly when you must slow down. If you slow down, you'll find that you actually will get more done because you'll make fewer mistakes and won't have to spend time on all of those do-overs. Take a few minutes first thing in the morning or at the end of the day and plan your day's or next day's activity. Make sure you prioritize your activity so you get what is most important done first and least important last. If it is the least, then it just might not matter if it gets done or not. Check out <u>First Things First</u> by Steven Covey, if you can find some time to read it. For those of you who can remember Simon and Garfunkel, I'm sure you'll remember one of their songs which told us to "Slow down, you move too fast. You got to make the morning last".

- It is difficult enough being responsible for our own problems. Don't try and be responsible for other people's problems when you have little or no control over them. It's great to listen and maybe even give some good advice, but don't accept ownership of other's problems.
- Minimize the negativity around you. We live in a world of 24/7 shock news. From the time we wake up and turn on the radio, TV, computer, cell phone or other device, we start getting bombarded with negative information about people, places and things happening around the world. We hear about the murders in our town and other towns around the country. We hear about the sexual assaults in

elementary, high school and on college campuses, sometimes by the very adults who have been given the authority to teach and supervise the students. We hear about the floods, hurricanes, tornadoes and other natural disasters that claim many lives and destroy whole cities or towns. We hear about the drug use in both amateur and professional sports. All this and also the daily run of the mill robberies, assaults, domestic abuse, fires and road rage incidents.

All of this negativity builds up and affects our day in such a bad way, that the few good things we hear about can't make a very positive impact on our lives. So I say to you, limit your exposure to TV, radio, movies, music and even negative or toxic people from whom you hear nothing but depressing news. Lay off the soaps and daytime talk shows that only promote low moral standards, degrading of other human beings and attempt to shock people to get higher ratings. Here are descriptions of seven types of toxic people who you should limit or eliminate time spent with them.

1. Manipulative – these individuals figure out what your "buttons" are, and push them to get what they want. They are experts at doing this, and you may not even know you are being manipulated until it is too late. They can make you do things you don't want to do and before you know it, you lose your sense of identity, your personal priorities and your ability to see the reality of the situation.

2. Narcissistic – these individuals have an extreme sense of self-importance and believe the world

revolves around them. These are the people who feel that "it's all about me". They solely focus on their own needs and not yours. They can leave you disappointed and unfulfilled. They zap your energy <u>by getting you to focus on them</u> and you have nothing left for yourself.

3. Downers – These individuals cannot appreciate the positives in life. If you say it is a beautiful day, they will tell you about the impending rainy forecast. If you are excited about your child graduating from high school, they will tell you about the high cost of college. These individuals take the joy out of everything. Your positive outlook continually gets squashed with their negativity and before you know it, their negativity consumes you and you start looking at life through their glasses.

4. Judgmental – If you find someone attractive, they will find something about them that is unattractive. If you find peoples' unique perspectives on life refreshing, they would find them just plain wrong. Spending a lot of time with them can inadvertently convert you into a judgmental person.

5. Dream Killers – These individuals will try to kill every idea or dream you have by telling you it is impossible. As you achieve at something, they will try to pull you down. They eat away at your self-esteem and your belief in yourself.

6. Insincere – You have an uncomfortable feeling around these people. If you have something exciting in your life, they react in a ho-hum way. If you are sad, they give you a "there, there" response. Or if you say something funny, they give you a polite smile or laugh. These individuals are building a

superficial relationship with you which is shallow and meaningless. When you really need a friend, they will not be there.

7. Disrespectful – These individuals will say or do things at the most inappropriate times and in the most inappropriate ways. They are more like subtle, grown up bullies. These people might use secrets that you have confided in them against you or stick their nose into your business when it is not wanted. They have no sense of boundaries and do not respect your feelings or your privacy. They can cause you to feel frustrated and disrespected.

You have a choice in all of this. You can turn them off completely or limit your exposure to them significantly. There are plenty of good TV programs, radio stations, movies, music and people that promote positive life styles. Search them out and turn them on. We've all heard that we can get cancer from second hand smoke. Well, you can also get second hand stress from listening to too much negativity.

- Trying to change the things you have no control over is futile. Accept what you can't change. Consider the Serenity Prayer, "**God, grant me the serenity to accept the things I can not change; courage to change the things I can; and wisdom to know the difference.**" Serenity means – calm and untroubled. To be without worry, stress or disturbance.

- Learn to say "no". This sounds like such an easy word to say and we've heard it since we were children. Why is it so hard for some people to use it to help from getting overburdened with responsibility? Here are a few ways to say no, without really saying no. These recommendations were provided by author William Ury from his book <u>The Power of a Positive No and Still Get to Yes</u>.

1. **Not now** - This softens the blow and keeps the door open for another time.
2. **I have another commitment** - No other excuse required. You honor your commitments.
3. **Maybe I can help you find someone who can** - This shows respect and concern. I do want to point out that this is not one that I would personally recommend. Committing to help someone find another person who can help them may take you more time than if you just did it yourself. I would use this as a last resort or just exclude this from the list. (Dan)
4. **I have a personal policy about**_____ - And fill in the blank. By saying this, you put the focus on a prior commitment to yourself without opening the door for an argument (useful, say when someone wants you to commit to working on Saturday or give to a charity when you have a different one in mind).
5. **I don't want to take on what I can't fully commit to doing well** - This is a yes to higher standards.

- Another hard thing for some people to do is to just "let go". General Colin Powell had a list of 10 rules to live by and one of them was to "get mad and get over it". But getting over it isn't always that easy. One of the first things you must do is to determine why you are hanging on to something before you can start to find a way to let go.
- Being assertive and asking for what you want and not what you don't want is important. In the book, <u>The Secret</u> by Rhonda Byrne, the author says that the secret to life is the Power of Attraction. She goes on to say that we need to ask for what we want and not what we don't want. We find this same message in I Kings 3:5 where God said to Solomon, "***ask for whatever you want me to give you***".

Here's an example that some of you may be able to relate to. I'm a golfer, or I should probably say that I like to play golf. For many years I would have thoughts during my round that I hope I didn't go into the water hazard or I don't want to go into the sand trap or the rough. I was thinking about what I didn't want. Now I say to myself, I want to hit it into the fairway or I want it to land on the green. See the difference? And yes, there was a difference in my golf game. I was hitting the fairway and greens more often and staying out of trouble more often. Another example would be to say I want to be healthy for the wedding this weekend instead of saying, I hope I don't get sick before the wedding this weekend. Think in the positive. Are we going to get everything we say we want? No I don't think it works that way, but putting positive thoughts rather than negative thoughts into our minds will generate more positive results.

- Accept your limits. I think that any of us can do anything that we want, but we just can't do everything we want. Set limits for what are really the important things in life and go after them. I often think of single parents in this case. They have to take on the role of both parents, hold down a job, take care of a home and still find time to have a life of their own. It is a big burden. When it gets tough, accept that you can't be super mom or super dad all the time and stop and ask for some help to get things back in order and get some time for yourself.

- Many people, including myself, have had or are harboring anger or even hatred toward another person for what they have done or we think they have done to us in the past. In almost every case, this anger or hatred is only hurting the person harboring those feelings and not the person that the anger or hatred is directed against. You are poisoning yourself. ***It's time to learn to forgive.***

Forgiving allows you to move out of the past and to start your life over with new hope. I recommend the book <u>Forgiveness is a Choice</u> by Robert Enright. I understand that some people have deep down feelings which you may have had for many years. You may have said many times that you could never forgive that person for what they did. Well, you must find a way because if you don't, you're just slowly killing yourself. Find the courage to move on.

If you read the introduction in this book, then you already know I served with the Marines in Vietnam. I am proud of being a Marine and I am proud that I served my country when they needed me. I would not change my decision to serve even if I could. However, what I did and what I saw had a very profound affect on me long after I returned.

For years I held feelings of anger and bitterness towards Vietnamese people and actually all Asians in general. I don't know why I grouped them together, but I did. So in the early 80's when the company that I was working for started hiring "these people", I wasn't too happy about it. I would see them in the hallway and I think they knew that I hated them. I would purposely walk toward them and try to forcefully bump into them. I was angry. I was wrong, but didn't know it yet.

Things changed one day when I was sent to Tokyo on business. The hotel had a nice "Scottish" style bar that attracted many businessmen and women. One afternoon when I returned from work, I stopped by for a drink. There were very few people there and so I pulled up a stool about 15 or 20 feet away from a young woman who was sitting at the end of the bar. After only a couple of minutes, the young lady spoke up saying, "Why do you hate me so much? I was just a baby when you were there."

The young lady happened to be Vietnamese. Since I had arrived at the bar, I had not looked at her other than at the moment I walked in and I had said nothing to her. Somehow, she knew that I had served in Vietnam during the war and that I felt anger towards her. Because of her "calling me out" and asking why I hated her when she was only a baby back then, my whole attitude changed. I realized that it wasn't her or the people of Vietnam or Asia that I hated. I hated what happened while I was there and how I was treated when I returned. It was then that I realized that it was time to forgive those who I thought were causing my anger and hatred and forgive myself for harboring these feelings for so long. I realized that my anger and hatred were only hurting me and that by forgiving, my life took a huge leap forward and went to a better place. There is a scripture that fits my situation to a T. Ezekiel 36:26 says: "*I will give you a new heart and put a new spirit in you. I will remove from you your heart of stone and give you a heart of flesh.*" That is exactly what happened.

- Relaxation should be a requirement in your daily life, not a luxury. There are a number of ways to relax. Here are four techniques you can use to help you relax.

The first technique is to breathe. When we were babies, we breathed from our diaphragm (stomach). Watch a baby sleeping today and see their stomach going up and down. For some reason, as we got older, we started breathing from our chest area. This works, but we get more oxygen into our bodies when we breathe from our diaphragm. So here are two breathing exercises that you can try for immediate stress reduction.

a. The balloon exercise – Get a balloon, take a big deep breath and blow into the balloon. You should feel an immediate release of your physical stress. Now, think about blowing up the balloon, but do it without the balloon. Take a deep breath in through your nose and then blow out hard through your mouth. Feel better? Women who have gone through natural child birth might know this exercise as a cleansing breath. Back in Chapter III, under Physical Symptoms, I spoke about the muscle tension we get driving. This breathing exercise will help eliminate that tension quickly.

b. 8-8-8 exercise – Get into a comfortable position: sitting, lying down or leaning up against a wall. Close your eyes and take a slow deep breath in to a count of 8. Hold it for 1 or 2 seconds and then release your breath slowly to a count of 8. Now do this 8 times (8-8-8). Maybe you don't have the lung capacity to do the 8 count. If not, try a 5-5-5 or 7-7-7 or whatever count is comfortable for you to use. If you are going to do this in your car, please pull over and park first before closing your eyes.

The second relaxation technique is a massage. Here are three categories of massage: Self, Friendship, Professional

1. Self massage -

Taking your thumb and index fingers, start at the top of your ear and gently massage down to the lobe. Do both ears for a minute or two each. Now move to your hands. Using your right hand, start massaging into the muscle area of the palm below your thumb and below the baby finger of your left hand. Now starting at the base of each finger and thumb of your left hand, massage and gently pull out towards the finger tips of each one. Switch and do the other hand. You may hear a popping sound as you gently pull past your knuckles. It was once thought that doing this could cause arthritis, but now we know that the noise is coming from gasses which have built up between the bones and it is not harmful. Recommendation: If you ever visit an Elder Care or Hospice Center, perform this exercise on the person you are visiting. They'll love it.

For the next self massage technique, go to the grocery store and buy a can of Campbell's soup. It doesn't matter what kind of Campbell's, but I do recommend Campbell's over other brands. Put the can on the floor, take off your shoes and run your feet over the can in a rolling motion. You are now giving yourself a foot massage. Feels good doesn't it? I recommend Campbell's soup brand because the cans have ridges and the ridges promote a better massage than non-ridged cans.

Another self massage recommendation involves a wine cork. Please don't think you have to drink an entire bottle of wine to get to the cork, but when you come upon a cork, save it. You may have to cut the cork ¼ or ½ inch to make it fit, but put the cork between your teeth and gently and steadily bite down on the cork. This action releases the pressure on your jaws and reduces the stress.

The final self massage is the rubber or squeeze ball exercise. If you don't have one, buy one. They don't cost much and they can be carried with you anywhere. Use the ball at any time by squeezing it in your hand, holding for a few seconds and then releasing. Do this several times using each hand. The tightening and releasing of the ball will reduce the stress in your muscles.

2. Friendship massage -

Sometimes it just feels better when someone else is doing the massaging. If you don't have the money for a professional massage, the friendship massage is a good alternative. A friend, of course, can also be a spouse. Really! Friendship massages should focus on four areas: the head, shoulders, hands and feet. Any of these can be done just about anywhere, anytime and doesn't take a lot of time to make a change in the way the recipient feels.

3. Professional massage -

The professional massage is normally delivered in two ways; the chair massage and the full body massage. Cost for these normally run about $1.00 per minute but I've seen ranges from $40 - $90 per hour for the full body type. Most of us can't afford or don't want to spend this amount of money on ourselves. However I do recommend that at some point you splurge and treat yourself. You might request a gift certificate for a massage on your next birthday, anniversary or for Christmas. You will have choices when you get there on what type of full body massage you want. There are the deep tissue and sports massages, therapeutic, aroma and hot rocks massages. For me, it is the old stand-by Swedish massage because it is gentle and relaxing. I walk away feeling better than when I walked in and after all, that is the purpose in the first place. I suggest you instruct your therapist to include your stomach muscles as part of the body massage.

A third relaxation technique is Visualization.

I like to refer to visualization as what Gilmore's mom told him in the movie Happy Gilmore as finding your happy place. We all can draw on something from our past that brings us joy and happiness. It might be as it is for me, to simply hold one of my grandsons in my arms while he is peacefully sleeping. Or even when one of them has birthday cake all over his face and enjoying every bit of it. Maybe you remember a particular sunrise or sunset while looking over a lake during one of your vacations. Maybe it is the beautiful snowcapped mountains in Denver during a ski trip or simply the love you see in your partner's eyes as you share a special moment with them. Just close your eyes (not while driving) and remember what your happy place experience was, breathe slowly, relax and enjoy the moment.

A fourth relaxation technique is Meditation.

There are many forms of meditation including prayer. I'll have more to talk about prayer later in the book. Most forms of meditation have a few things in common. They all tell you to get into a comfortable position, close your eyes, and clear your mind by focusing on your breathing. Some will tell you to think about and repeat a word or phrase such as "ohme" or "I am at peace". This is so you can drive out all of the other chatter we often have in our minds that keep us from relaxing. Try it. It doesn't take long and again, you can do it most anywhere.

- Now for one of the most rewarding tips I can give to anyone, especially to men. It is OK to cry. Yup, cry. As boys growing up, many of us were told not to cry, that only girls cry and crying is for sissies. Well, I guess that makes me a sissy. In the introduction to this book, I told you that something important happened in 1986 that I would tell you about later. Well, it's later. I had been using many of the techniques that I had learned to manage my stress. But there was still something inside me that was not letting me get to that comfortable place, that happy place. I finally figured out what it was. It had been four years since my doctor told me that I needed to talk about the things in my life I had been suppressing, specifically the deaths in my family, Vietnam and the guilt about traveling and spending so much time away from my family.

One evening in the summer of 1986, I asked my wife if she would come out on our deck (**Deck Night**) and listen while I shared some things that were troubling me. That evening we spent four or five hours on the deck, and during that time I spilled out all sorts of things that were ripping me apart inside. God bless her, my wife just listened. I shed tears by the buckets that night and so much anger, bitterness, frustration, guilt and hatred was lifted out of me and washed away. From that point on in my life, I found it much easier to talk about anything that was causing me pain and I found it much easier to cry. And guess what? I'm no sissy! I was giving a talk in North Carolina when one of the attendees raised their hand and said, "I don't have a deck, will my front porch work"? Yes, a front porch will do just fine.

- According to medical studies, changing from an inactive to active lifestyle through physical activity can decrease your odds of premature death by 24%. When you don't exercise, your muscles let out a trickle of chemicals that tells every cell day after day to decay. Nike, through their marketing of "Just Do It," changed the lifestyle of many people and new commercials from the American Heart Association tell us to "Do walk, run, swim, garden, golf, bowl, etc." You don't have to spend two hours a day at the gym to make a difference in your stress levels. Do something for 30 minutes once a day and see the difference.
- Getting involved by helping others is another way to reduce stress levels. According to recent research, a person who helps someone out gets as much benefit from doing so as the person being helped. A chemical called serotonin is released in our bodies which is a chemical that makes us feel good. In the studies, the same amount of serotonin was released

in the giver of the good deed as was in the recipient of the good deed.

- Laugh at and be nice to yourself. Most of us take life way too seriously. We have to learn to accept the fact that we are not perfect and we do things that don't always make a lot of sense. We need to start treating ourselves as if we are our own best friend. It has been said that during a press conference with Abraham Lincoln, a reporter called the President two-faced. President Lincoln looked at the reporter and said, "If I was two-faced, do you think I would be wearing this one?"

- Put some fun in your life. That's the theme of the Mall of America in Bloomington, Minnesota. It should be everyone's theme. Go to a funny movie. Visit the zoo. Be silly. Spend some time with someone who makes you laugh. What did the snail say while riding on the back of the turtle? Weeeeeee!

- Improve your relationship with God. In the next chapter you will be provided with scripture from the Old and New Testament which may be helpful to get through serious situations. Use the Bible as your ultimate stress management reference book. When I first started giving talks on this subject, my wife came to me and said that her Christian group would like me to come to one of their monthly meetings and speak. She asked if I could give my program using Christian references. I said "sure" I can. I really didn't know how because at the time, I really wasn't what I would consider a good Christian, although I did go to church occasionally.

I was traveling for my job one Sunday morning and got to the airport my usual two hours before my flight. I don't normally do this, but on this particular morning, I decided to stop at one of the coffee shops and have a cup of coffee and a donut. Being that it was Sunday morning, the TV in the coffee shop was tuned into a Christian station. As I looked up, I saw the picture of an eagle and the preacher was saying, "and soar on his strength". Then it hit me. I am a huge fan of the American Bald Eagle. I know that the eagle perches itself on the highest tree or mountain top and when it is ready to fly, it simply steps off the tree branch or cliff and opens its wings. The eagle knows that when it does this, there will be wind that will collect under its wings that will allow it to soar. So I had my inspiration. ***"Trust in the Lord and Soar on His Strength"***

- Taking care of yourself is extremely important. As I had written earlier, you must take care of yourself first before you can help others. This includes eating right, getting the proper rest, exercise, and taking care of yourself spiritually.
- Getting a good night's sleep is very important. As we sleep, our body recovers from the stresses of the day. If we are not sleeping or sleep is frequently interrupted, we are losing an opportunity to recover. Here are some ways we can improve the likelihood of a good night's rest.

a. Keep the briefcase and family problems out of the bedroom. If you can't stop thinking about work or family issues, get up and write down what is troubling you.
b. Keep the room as dark as possible; and if this is difficult to do, wear eye covers to darken the room.
c. Relax before trying to sleep by using one of the relaxation techniques described in this book.
d. Go to bed and wake up at the same time each day.
e. Stretch and ease out of bed in the morning.

- Finally we end with attitude. I think *it is extremely important to "choose" to have a good attitude every day*. I do believe that we get to choose whether we are going to have a good day or a bad day. Everything you do this day will take a different path depending on your choice to have a good day or not. Are there people who choose to have a bad day? Believe it or not, there are, and most don't even know they are asking for it. Remember to "ask for what you want, not what you don't want?" So ask for a good day. Choose this type of attitude and see your life improve. Each of you has talents, abilities and potentials. By learning to appreciate these and not worrying about mistakes you may have made this day, you will choose to have a better attitude about life. Choose to like yourself and catch yourself doing things right. Many people make themselves a "to do list". That is all well and good. However, along with this, try making yourself an "I did list". Let yourself see all of the things you accomplished during the day. If you deal with children as a parent, grandparent, teacher, day care provider or in any other way, try to remember to catch them doing things right instead of harping on the things they do wrong. Get them started on a life of being positive about who they are.

Special **Holiday Stress** Management Tips

1. Breathe - deeply, completely, and often.
2. Delegate - don't try to do everything yourself.
3. Express - your expectations clearly (We need to be at the airport by 3, so we need to be in the car and on our way by 1:30.)
4. Focus - on the real meaning of the holiday!
5. Just Say No! – don't let others overload you. Practice saying no using one of the alternative phrases shared earlier in this book.
6. Kiss - the one you love.
7. Let go - of unrealistic expectations.
8. More - is not necessarily better. Keep things as simple as you can.
9. Nap - when your body tells you to rest and recharge.
10. Unwind - with a massage, a manicure, or even a long, hot bath.
11. Walk - in the sunshine for a few minutes each day to get some natural vitamin D.
12. Review your priorities - Decide in advance where to best invest your time and energy.
13. Sleep - Schedule at least seven hours of sleep. Most disagreements start when someone is overtired.

So let's summarize the tips:

Learn the signs of stress
Utilize resources available to you
Slow Down
Reduce your exposure to negativity
Accept what you can not change
Learn to say no
Learn to let go
Ask for what you want
Accept your limits
Learn to forgive
Learn to relax
    Slow breathing
    Massage
    Visualization
    Meditation and Prayer
Let yourself cry
Exercise
Volunteer to help others
Laugh and be nice to yourself
Put some fun into your life
Improve your relationship with God
Take care of yourself
Get a good night's sleep
Choose to have a good attitude and
    appreciate yourself

––––––––––––

Chapter V:
Biblical Helps

In this chapter I've provided the location for you to find the words in the Bible to help you through life's situations. I could have given you the actual scripture instead of just the location. However, I found out on my own that it is better to pick up the Book and look it up myself, rather than having someone do it for me.

Reducing Negative Feelings

Anxiety
Psalm 46:1
Psalm 55:22
Psalm 94:18–19
Philippians 4:6–8
I Peter 5:6, 7

Bitterness
Ephesians 4:31, 32
Ezekiel 36:26
James 1:2–4

Depression
Psalm 34:1–4
Psalm 42:5
Psalm 69:1
Psalm 71:3, 20, 21

Disappointment in Friends
Psalm 41:9–13

II Timothy 4:16–18

Discouragement	Psalm 42:6–11
	II Corinthians 4:8–12
	Psalm 69:1
Doubt	Matthew 8:26
	Jude: 22
	James 1:6
	Mark 11:23
	John 20:27
	Matthew 14:31
	Matthew 21:21
Fear	Matthew 10:28
	Hebrews 13:5, 6
	Psalm 27:1
	Psalm 71:3
Grief	Matthew 5:4
	II Corinthians 1:3, 4
	John 11:25, 26
	Psalm 31:7–10
Homesickness	Psalm 121
Loneliness	Psalm 23
	Hebrews 13:5, 6
	Matthew 28:20
Sorrow	Matthew 5:4
	John 11:25, 26
	Jeremiah 31:12
	Psalm 31:7–10, 14–16

Temptation	Psalm 1
	Matthew. 26:41
	I Corinthians 10:13
	Hebrews 2:18
Weariness	Psalm 69: 1
	Matthew 11:28-30
	Psalm 90:1–6, 13–17
Worry	Matthew 6:19–34
	I Peter 5:6, 7
	Luke 12:25

Sometimes it seems that God will use stress to show us where and what we need to work on in our lives. Take some time to ask God what He wants to show or teach you.

Increasing Positive Attitudes

Assurance of Salvation	John 3:16
	Romans 8:1, 2
	Philippians 1:6
Attitude	Philippians 4:8
	Colossians 3:2
Contentment	I Timothy 6:6
	Matthew 6:19–21
	Philippians 4:11–13
Courage	Psalm 27:1–5
Faith	Matthew 8:5–13
	Ephesians 2:8, 9
Forgiveness	Mark 11:25, 26
	Luke 23:34
	Psalm 32:1–5
	Psalm 103:12
	I John 1:9
	Colossians 3:13
	Isaiah 1:18
	Matthew 18:21, 22
	Isaiah 55:6–8
Happiness/Joy	Matthew 5:11–12
	Philippians 4:4
	Psalm 37:4
	Luke 10:20

Hope	I Peter 1:13
	Psalm 42:5
	Psalm 71:20–21
	Isaiah 40:31
Love	I Corinthians 13:1–8,13
Patience	Hebrews 10:36
	Galatians 6:9
Peace with God	John 14:27
	John 16:33
	Romans 5:1, 2
	Philippians 4:7
Resolution	Ephesians 6:10–18
Sincerity	Philippians 1:9, 10
Victory	I Corinthians 15:57
	Psalm 21:1
	Psalm 60:12

This might be a good place to reiterate the words of the Serenity Prayer which many find helpful when they find themselves worrying too much.

"**God – Grant me the serenity to accept the things I can not change, courage to change the things I can and wisdom to know the difference**."

Serenity means – calm and untroubled. To be without worry, stress or disturbance.

———————

Chapter VI:
Summary

One key to successfully managing the stress in your life is to create a balanced lifestyle. Think of it as Chart D shows below. We have 168 hours in a week, and there are a number of components which take up our time during that week. Look at your life and determine where you're spending most of your time. For many of you who are still in the workforce, work will fill most of your weekday and maybe evening time. But are you finding time for all of the other components of your life that makes up who you are? Ideally you'll want some time spent in each of the components shown, and sometimes that can't always be accomplished. But that should be your goal. **Balance in your life is the key**.

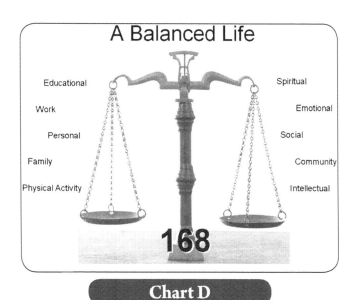

Chart D

Since "**Deck Night**", so many years ago, I have continued my research on methods and techniques to reduce stress and enhance my overall well being. During this time, I have also lost two more family members. In 1999, my mother Anna passed away at the age of 80. She died of a stroke. Then in 2004, my brother Jerry, at age 60, died of a heart attack. Yes, there is a cycle of life and it does include death. I once heard that it is not the birth and death date on your tombstone that signifies our lives, but the dash (-) between the two dates. Make the most of that dash and *aim to make every day of your life the best day of your life.*

Before I end this book, I want to share with you one of my favorite poems written by Anna Quindlen

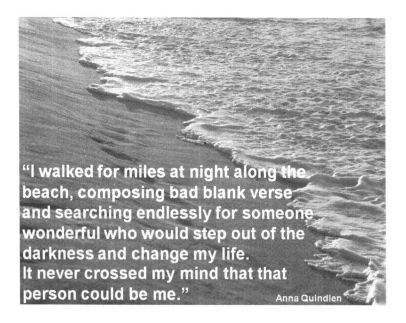

"I walked for miles at night along the beach, composing bad blank verse and searching endlessly for someone wonderful who would step out of the darkness and change my life. It never crossed my mind that that person could be me."
Anna Quindlen

You are the only one who can make the changes to improve your life, and the time to start is now. And as that internationally known author by the name "Unknown" once wrote: **"Don't ask God to guide your footsteps if you aren't willing to move your feet".**

Chapter VII:
References

The following books have influenced my philosophy on stress management -

From Burnout to Balance

- Jaffe and Scott

Staying Alive

- Michael McKinley

7 Habits of Highly Successful People and
First Things First

- Steven Covey

Celestine Prophecy

- James Redfield

Play the Game (Golf and Life)

- Sheard and Armstrong

10 Secrets for Success and Inner Peace

- Wayne Dyer

The Power of Focus

- Jack Canfield

The Travelers' Gift

- Andy Andrews

Claiming your Place at the Fire

- Leider and Shapiro

The Blessing

- Smalley and Trent

Idiot's Guide to Managing Stress

- Jeff Davidson

Feel the Fear and Do it anyway

- Susan Jeffers

Managing Stress in a Changing World

- Susan Balfour

Stress Busters

- Katherine Butler

Stress Free for Good

- Luskin and Pelletier

Forgiveness is a Choice

- Robert Enright

The Secret

- Rhonda Byrne

The Four Agreements

- Don Miguel Ruiz

The Holy Bible

- NIV

Breaking Free from Stress

- Linda Mintle PHD

Daily Relaxer
- Mathew McKay and Patrick Fanning

Body and Soul magazine

The Five Love Languages
- Chapman and Thomas

The Power of a Positive No and Still Get to Yes
- William Ury

The following speakers have influenced my philosophy on stress management -

Karen Kaiser Clark
Dr. Wayne Dyer
Chris Christianson
Mike McKinley
Mike Podolinsky
Kenneth Crockford
Colin Powell
Steven Covey
Joyce Meyer

Internet References -

National Institute of Health
Caremark Health Resources Studies
National Institute of Health
Duke University
University of Washington Medical School
Christian Answers